The water slide

Story by Annette Smith
Illustrations by Trish Hill

One Saturday morning,

Tim's mom said,

"We are going on a picnic today."

"Oh, good," said Tim.

"Can Michael come with us?"

"Yes," said Mom.

"You can call him.

Tell him to bring

his swimming things."

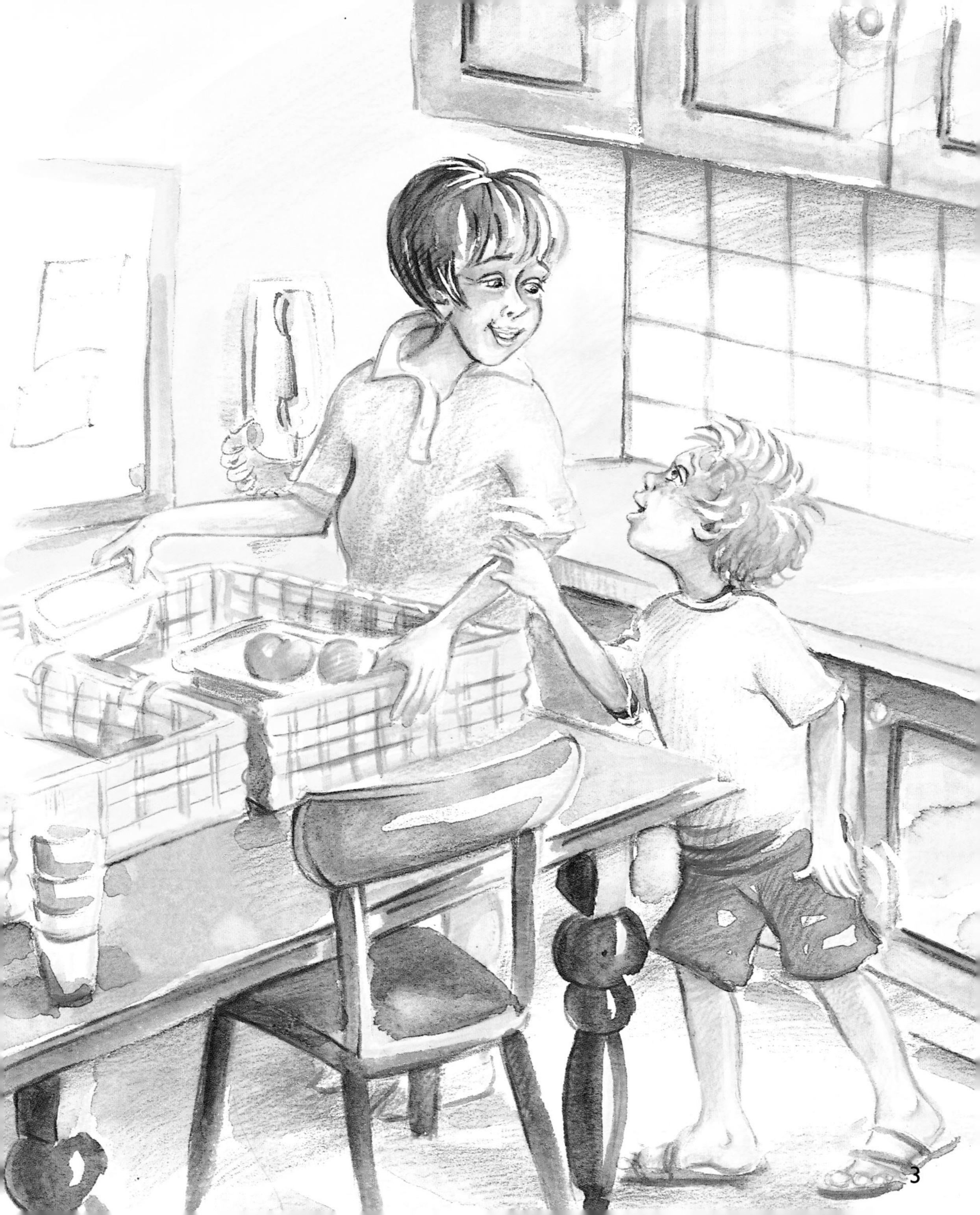

"We are going to have fun today,"
said Tim.

"Where are we going?" said Michael.

"Mom and Dad won't tell me,"
laughed Tim.
"They are taking us
to a new park."

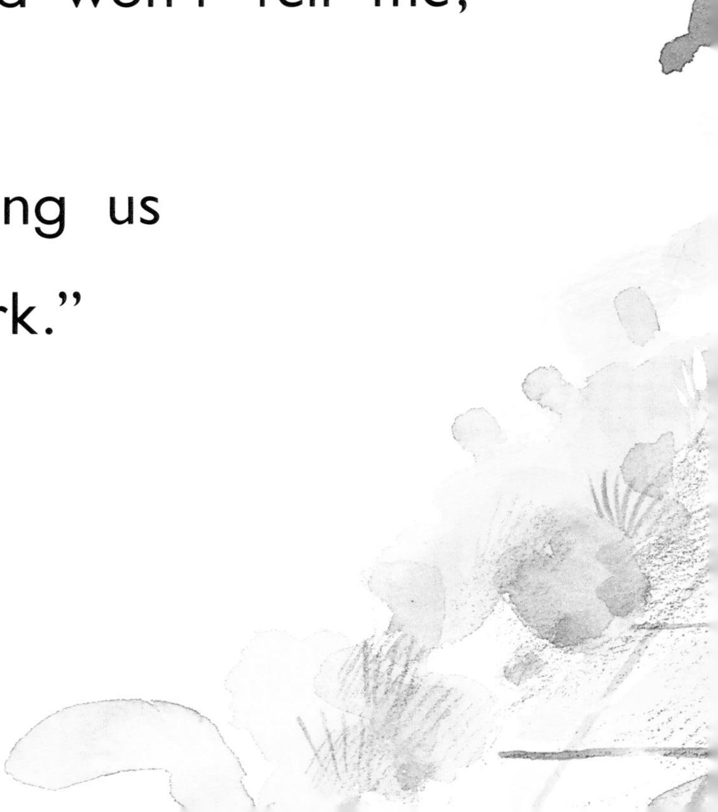

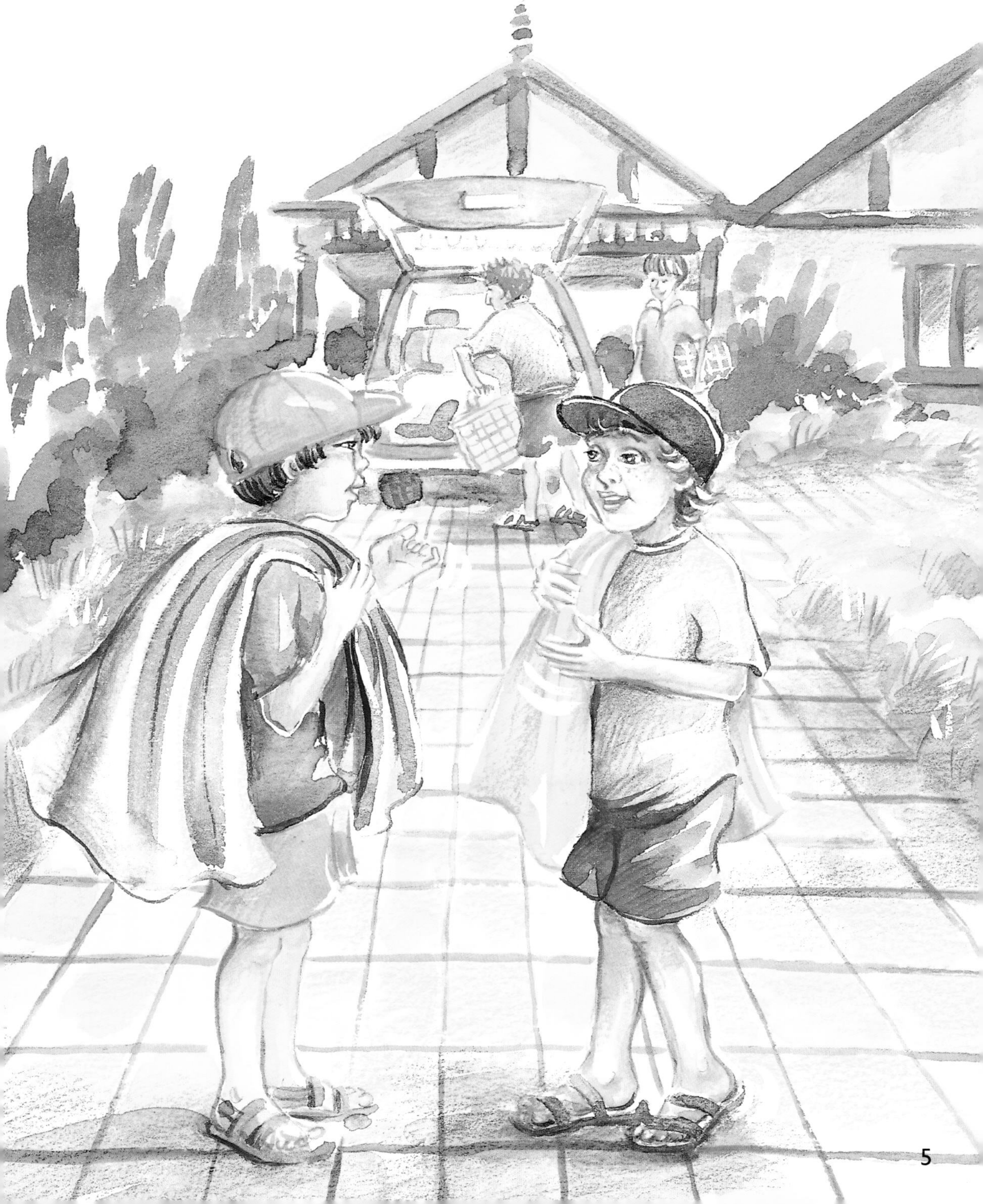

They drove all the way
past the stores.
Then Tim's dad stopped the car
outside a park.

"Tim," said Michael,
"look over there.
This park has a swimming pool
and a **water slide**, too."

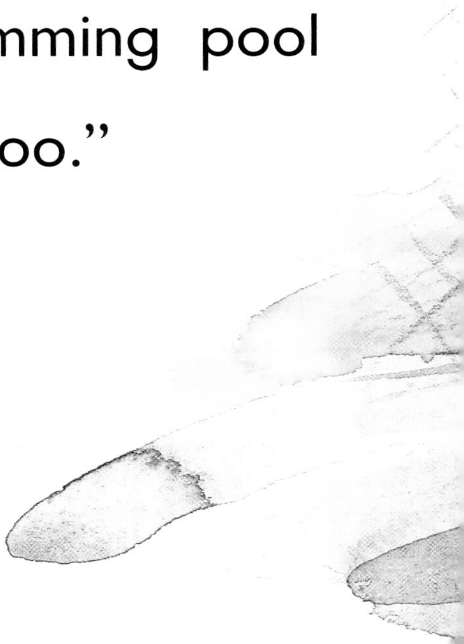

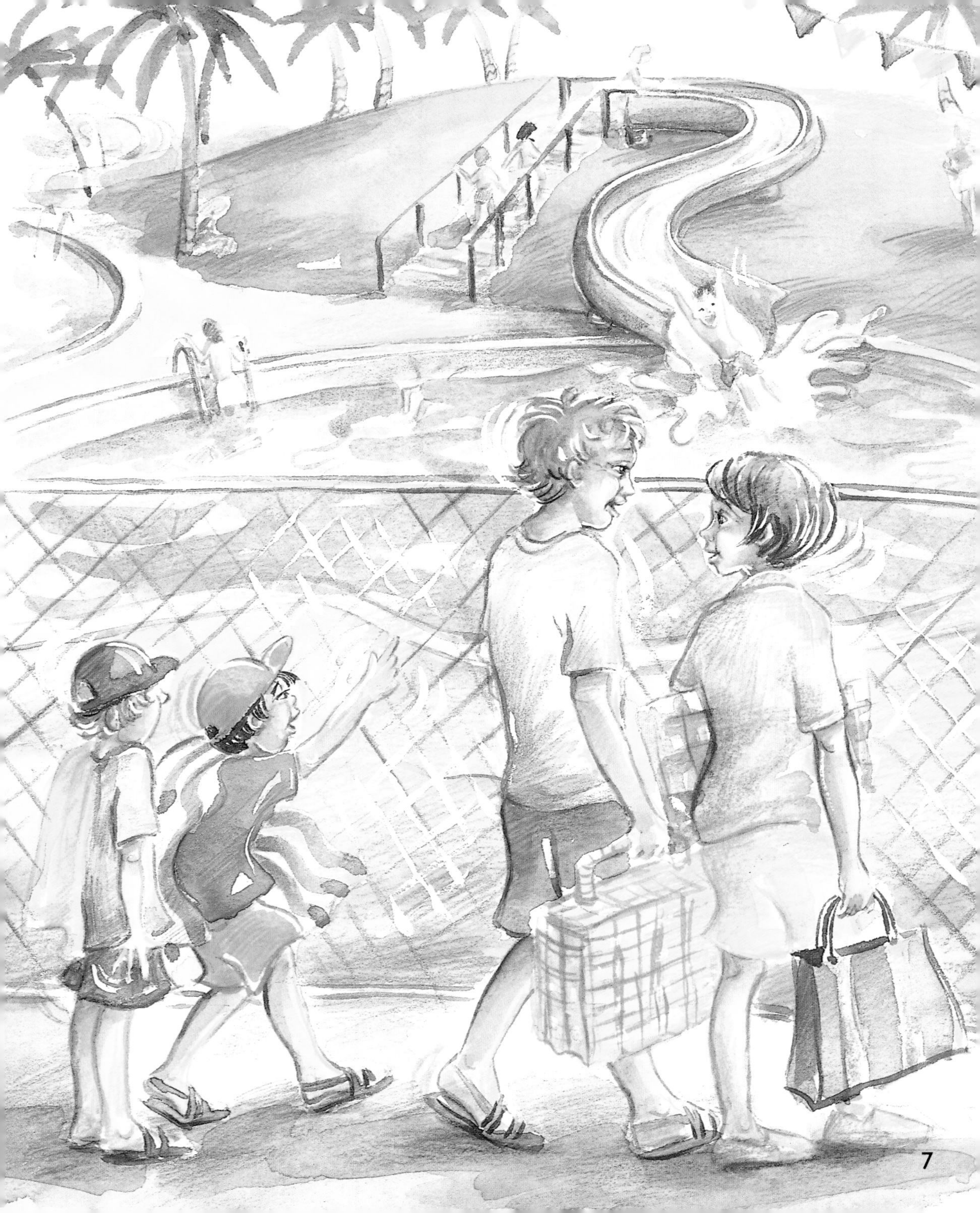

"Oh, no," said Tim.
"That slide looks too big for me.
I don't want to go on it."

"Come on, Tim," shouted Michael.

"You go first," said Tim.
"I will swim here with Dad."

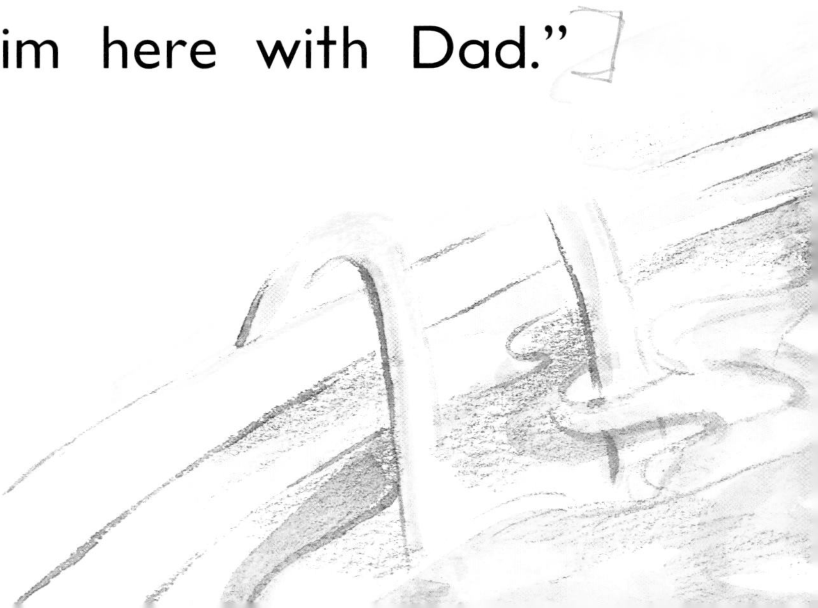

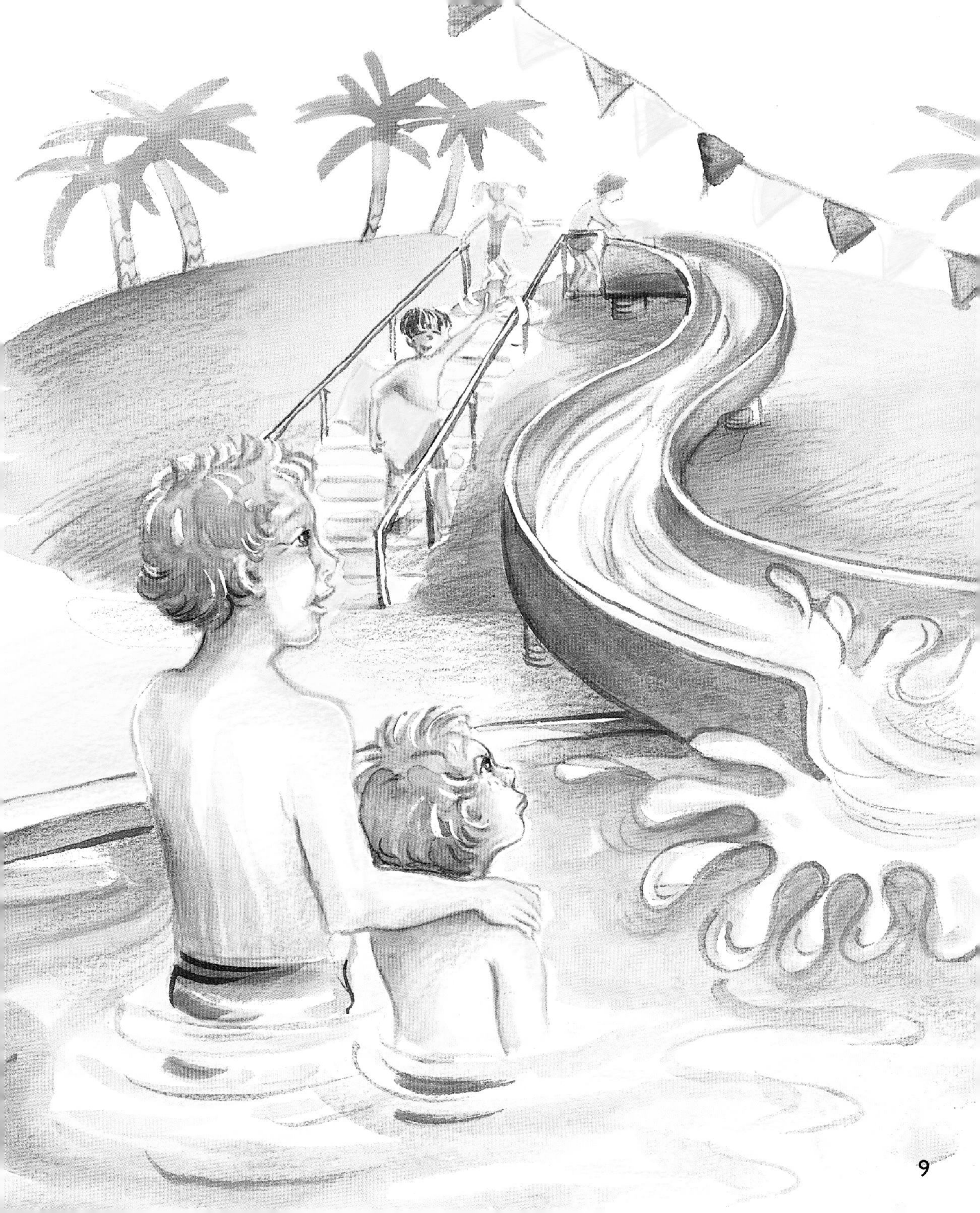

Michael went down the water slide lots of times.

"Dad," said Tim,
"Michael is having fun on the slide.
I want to have a turn now."

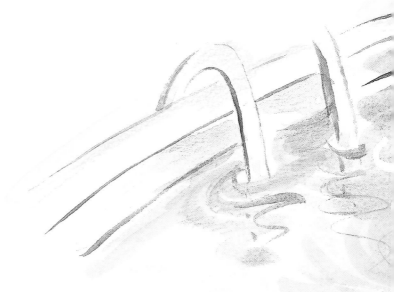

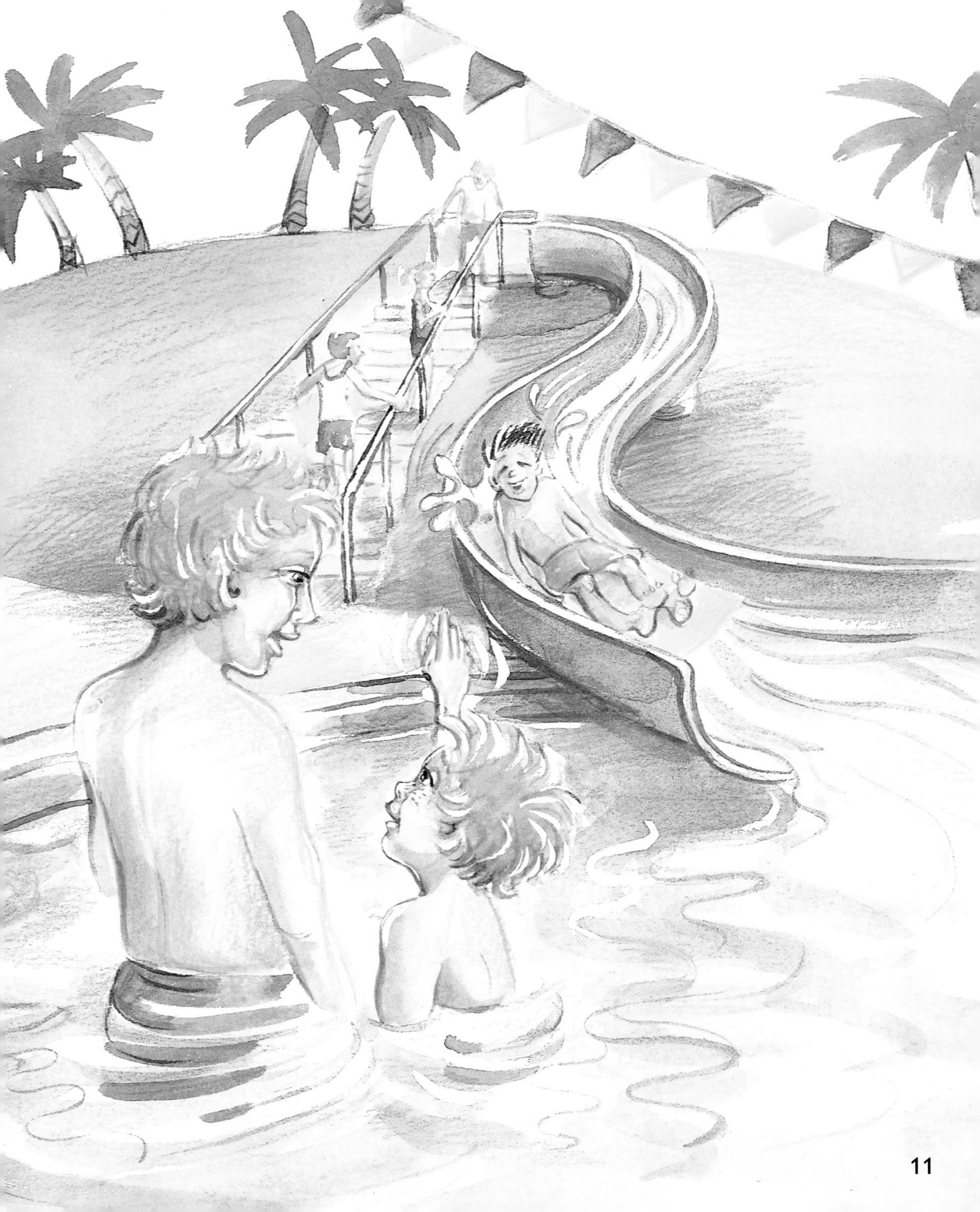

Tim climbed up the steps
to the top of the water slide.

"Tim," said Michael,
"come and sit here on my mat.
You can come down with me
this time."

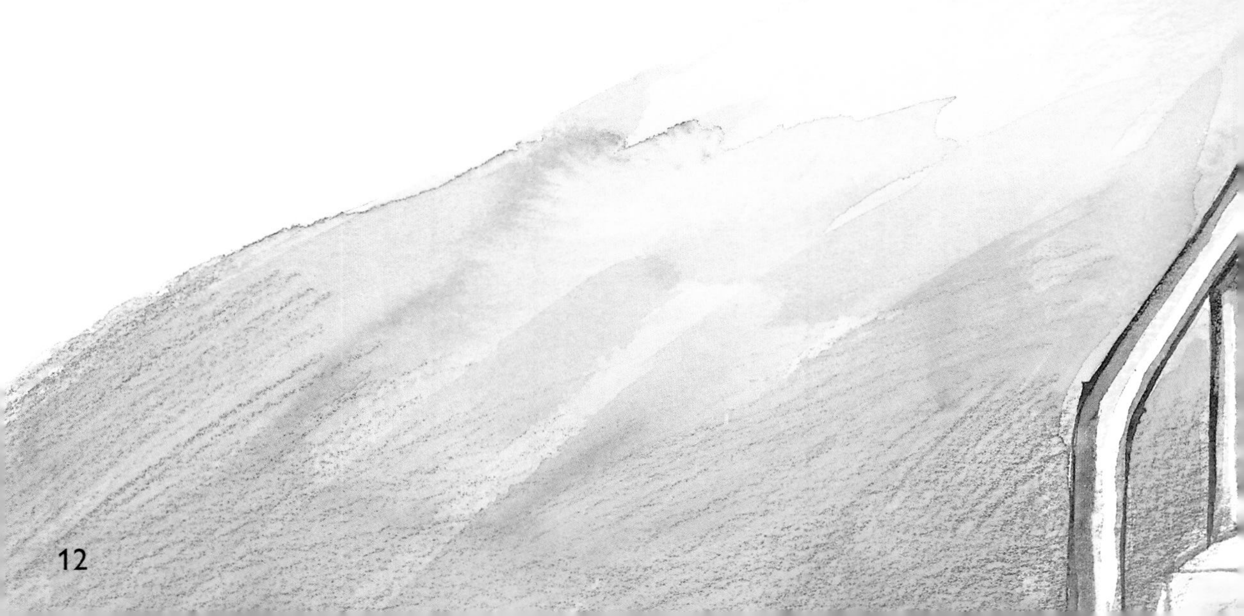

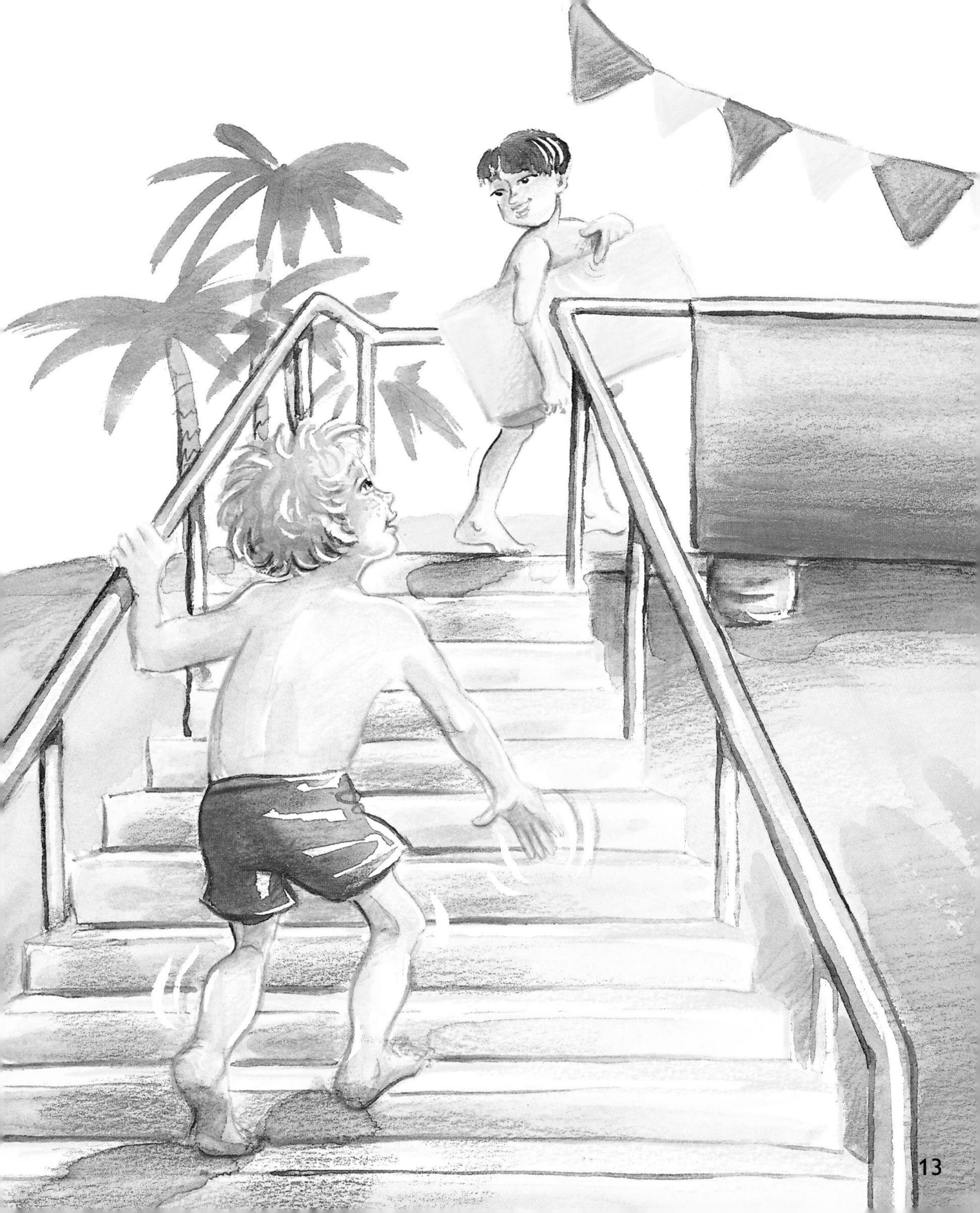

The boys went slowly at first.
Then they went faster and faster
down the slide and into the water.

Tim laughed as they climbed
out of the pool.
"That was fun," he said.

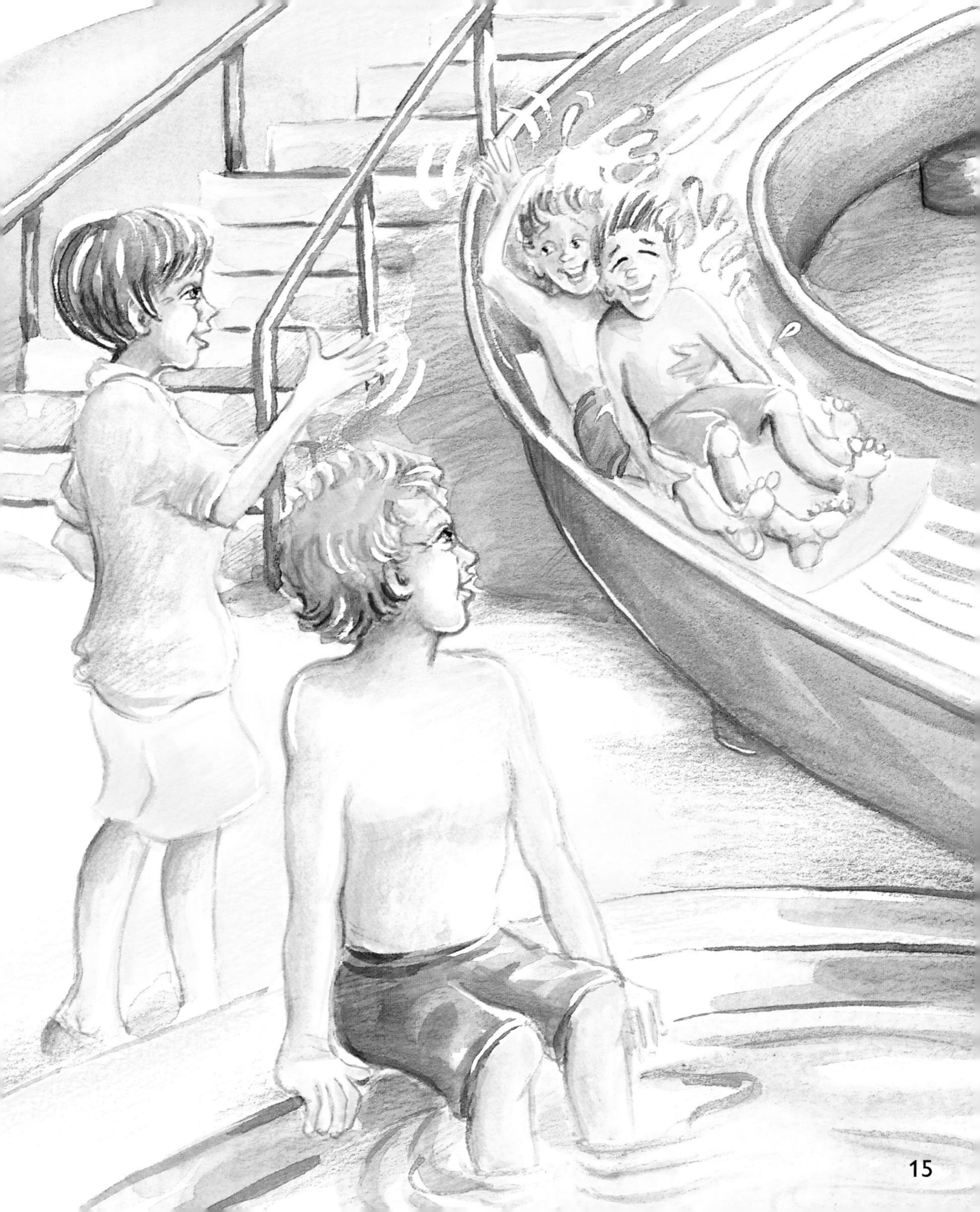

"I'm going to have a turn by myself now," said Tim.

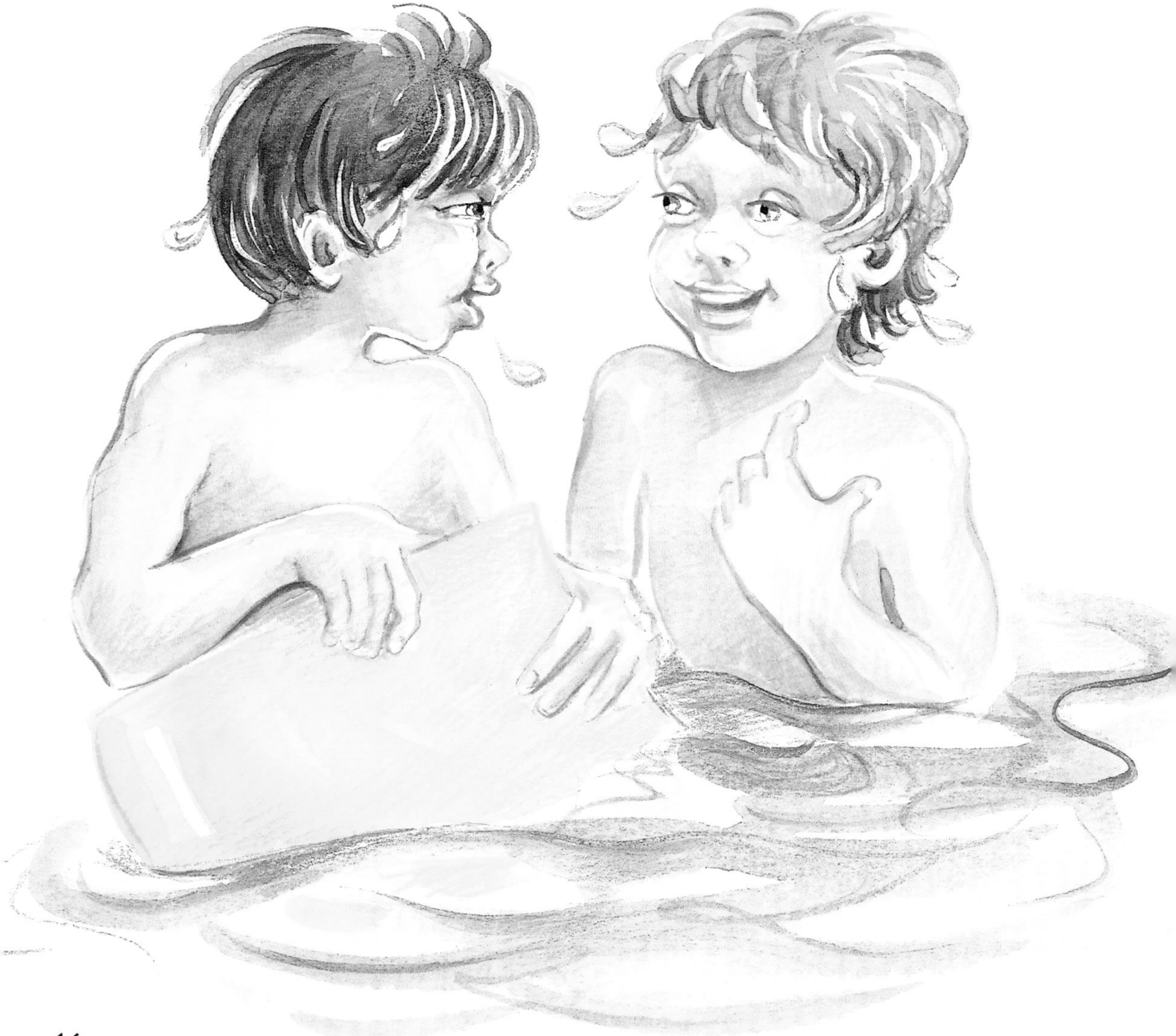